Today I Baled Some Hay to Feed the Sheep the Coyotes Eat

WITHDRAWN

Today I Baled Some Hay
To Feed the Sheep
the Coyotes Eat

Text and
Drawings by

Published by

FALCON
PRESS
PUBLISHING CO. INC.

Library of Congress Catalog Card Number: 83-81970

ISBN 0-934318-26-3

Manufactured in the United States of America

Falcon Press Publishing Co., Inc.
  Editorial and production: P.O. Box 731, Helena, MT 59624
  Marketing and distribution: P.O. Box 279, Billings, MT 59103

To my wife Elvia, who has "licked" her share of lambs...and scrubbed my muddy footsteps from the kitchen floor...and washed my slimy coveralls...and above all, simply put up with me during all these years.

Contents

Foreword

"I was dropped in Minnesota, but born in Montana," artist-sheepman Bill Stockton, Grass Range, says of himself.

Stockton, son of Fergus County homesteaders, grew up in central Montana. His education included stays at several colleges and art study in Paris, France. A European tour of duty during the Second World War netted him a philosophy of life and art, which he is constantly updating, and a charming French wife whom he transplanted from her native Paris to a sheep spread near Grass Range, Montana. They have two sons.

Stockton's art—running a range from signs, furniture, and light fixtures to abstract-expressionist paintings and his widely known metal sculpture—is displayed in private homes, museums, and art galleries in the U.S. and Europe.

Described by the editor of the state's leading newspaper as "perhaps the finest artist Montana has produced since Charlie Russell," Stockton is currently working on a watercolor series—when he can take time away from his sheep ranching duties, which, he proudly points out, produce food and clothing for people.

There is a lot of information in this book about sheep; there is even more information about people—about the men like Bill who battle the elements, the animals, and themselves to provide all of us with food and clothing; and about the rest of the human population—the "dudes", who take so much (and take so much for granted) from the farmer and rancher—and give so little, even in the way of understanding, in return.

In the course of many visits with Bill and his lovely wife Elvia, at their Grass Range ranch, I've discovered—and am still discovering—the many facets of the man who authored this manuscript. And through his work, the same opportunity is available to you.

You'll learn a lot about sheep from this book; you'll laugh at some parts and probably be shocked or sickened by others. You'll enjoy the drawings. But this book will do more than amuse you or give you moments of enjoyment or teach you about sheep. It will teach you something about yourself.

Sue Mathews
Eastern Montana College
Billings, Montana

Preface

I dedicate this book to all those people who have never experienced the commoness of death, birth, and the uncommoness of life; to all those people who have never been out in ten-below weather extracting a rotted fetus from a mother ewe.

The snow is a foot deep; the wind continues to blow, and the sheep have given no sign that the weather will break soon. The storm is not usual or unusual for April; it, like death, is part of the sheep business.

The ewe has used up all the lubricants of birth, but I manage to dig out the lamb by ripping off one front leg. The brown, rotted slime is all the way to my elbow. I wipe some of it away in the snow and I go in after the other twin, hoping it might be alive. It isn't.

Ironically, in all this, the only parts of my body which remain warm are my hands and the forearms. The pressures inside the vagina are such that they weaken one's arm within seconds, and it is necessary to alternate—what the right hand can't manipulate, the left hand manages.

Welcome to the terrible, wonderful life of raising sheep.

...I wrote this preface to my notebook several years ago with no plans of it ever being printed. It all started as a notebook of drawings with observations and comments thrown in. The comments just kept on growing; some to chapters, others to newspaper articles.

Anyway, this book is about sheep. Oh no, it is not about the lonely shepherd, his wagon and dog, or the exotic Basque trailing his flocks to the mountain. No, it is about sheep: the "cleft-footed locust" as former Secretary of the Interior Stewart Udall called them.

It is about a soft-dispositioned, pacific mammal that so many people hate (because they are pacific, probably) and very few understand. It is about a beautiful, timid animal who, for centuries, has clothed and fed millions and millions of human beings; an animal that has now become one of the diminishing species in America.

This book is about the problems of being a sheep and a few of the problems of the people who care for them. It is about the sheep's enemies: the predators, the weather, and man.

Bill Stockton
Grass Range, Montana
February, 1974

How It All Started

T HE little lamb was quite unaware of his ground
level protrusion into this world; nor was he able
to see, even from the heighth of 15 inches as his mother
stood up to drop him, through the translucent membrane that enveloped him. His mind was not activated
until he gasped his first breath of air.

*Nature purposely gave me
long legs so I could reach my
mother's tits. But wouldn't
it have worked just
as well if nature
had made my legs
shorter and
my mother's
udder closer
to the
ground?*

The lamb's head flopped from side to side as his mother hurriedly licked away the membrane. He now felt for the first time the temperatures of spring, and saw the few square feet of his first place on earth. What thoughts he might have had deep within his mother were now forgotten as his new intelligence awakened him to the obligations of survival.

For the first minutes, his long legs refused any of the normal commands of his mind; but he kept on trying, aided by the licking and bunting of his mother. Soon he managed to support himself on one hind leg, and then the other. For him this was a great achievement, so he rested awhile and surveyed that part of the world he could see from a vantage point of six inches above the earth.

His front legs were a bigger problem, since they bent in a different direction; when he did manage to get them straightened out, the hind legs collapsed, and he had to start all over. But, at last, propped up by his mother's nose as she licked his naval, he negotiated his first four-legged stand in the world.

The trip to the tit was now the big task ahead for the little lamb. Guided by the intelligence given him a few seconds after birth, he understood that there was a source of life-giving milk somewhere near his mother's leg—which leg, he was not sure. But he knew that it was about 14 inches from the ground and that he would have to raise his head to find it. This is all he really knew, but it would prove to be enough.

The little lamb bunted and tasted all of the areas beneath his mother's brisket and between her front legs. Once, he was sure he had found the tit, but it turned out to be nothing but a wet strand of wool. "Strange," he mused to himself, "it could have been there as well as any other place."

The mother now came to the lamb's rescue; with her nose, she gently pushed and guided him on the wobbly journey back to her rear. He stopped from time to time to examine all the likely places on his mother's underneath and to gaze out at that vast environment

6

called world. But the driving instincts within him reoriented any notions he might have had to explore that strange country out there, and the search for the nourishment continued. It took two trips around his mother's hindlegs and a slight entanglement with his mother's afterbirth before he found that elusive tit. But there it was—right where he had been informed it should have been.

The little lamb sucked as fast as he could, since he felt that this was a very important thing to do. He wagged his tail in double time, as a signal to his mother that everything was going well. His mother licked his hindlegs and from time to time beneath his tail, just to reassure herself of ownership. For her it had been a desperate half hour and now it was over. Unlike last year when her lamb had gone down in a blizzard, she now had a baby to nurse for the rest of the spring and summer months.

Pages from my Notebook

IT all starts with a fertilized seed, so if one ram is turned out with fifty ewes on the first day of December, one ewe will lamb the 26th of April, one the 27th, one the 28th, two the 29th, two the 30th, three the first of May, and so on until about the 27th of May, when there will only be left to lamb one barren "old girl" who has never in her five years of life enjoyed the sentiments of motherhood.

I think I'll start breeding sheep with smaller heads and foreheads. This is where the big stretch is for an old ewe—getting the forehead past the "Whatcha-ma-calllit."

Note: Certainly, if I were a young girl with dreams of motherhood and in search of a young man, I would carry a set of calipers in my purse and measure the handsome skulls of all my suitors.

Not even an obstetrician, who has delivered a hundred babies or so, could have empathy with a rancher and his struggle to relieve a mother animal of her young with the aid of levers and pullies, all without the benefits of anaesthetics of any sort. I guess, though, that this is not the place to be facetious. In later pages, I shall write about this.

AN old ewe, if she is aware that someone is watching her lamb, will urinate very often and most certainly postpone the event for at least a half hour or longer.

I had always assumed that once nature had triggered the motions of birth, hell or high water couldn't stop them. But such is not the case. An old ewe, when she's interrupted, will stand up and then very calmly start chewing her cud. She'll wander off to a new location, hoping, of course, she won't be followed. Again, she'll probably squat a couple of times in another effort to convince you that nothing more eventful was going to happen than the usual four-hour pee-break.

OH yes, in case my good readers might wonder if I don't know what a sheep looks like, here is a drawing of a prize Rambouillet yearling ewe in all her woolen finery.

(B UT I guess only I would recognize her beautiful fibers draped over the back
of some knocked-kneed, New York
"broad" in the form of a
$400.00 coat.

Strange, but for the ewe, her
$5.00 fleece served only the
function of warmth, while
for the urban female, it
serves only the function
of sophistication.

...And the yearling was
quite unaware of how
lovely she really was.)

B ACK to sheep:
After a sheep is sheared, her anatomy is exposed
and she, therefore, has more character and is more interesting to draw.

For example, here is a drawing of a spindle-legged,
"pot-gutted," five-year-old ewe who would win a prize
nowhere except maybe at the bank.

I F I were called on to give advice to someone
inspired to go into the sheep business, I would say
to avoid at all costs a sheep with no belly. A sheep is a

ruminant animal designed to consume large quantities of roughage. She, therefore, is in need of a large "plant" that can convert sagebrush, chokecherry leaves, bunch grass, alfalfa and any and all kinds of weeds into milk, lambs and wool. In this factory process there is usually very little left for the ewe's maintenance. For this reason, a good producing ewe is never fat—take away the "gut" and there is little left.

The varying shapes of pregnancies.
May be the one on the left will
be twins — maybe not.

P regnancies take on many shapes, but the only
  real judgment one can make of the expected event
is to have seen the ewe bred, count the days, look up
her past history (which is usually impossible) and then
hope she'll do as well, or better, this time around.

All ranchers, cattlemen or sheepmen, are guilty of the
wrong prognosis when anticipating an animal's time to
give birth. This is important since we might have to be
prepared to help deliver her young, or to bring her to
shelter. We try to read the signs: such as the fullness of
the abdomen, size of the udder, the looseness around
the vulva, etc. But unless the ewe is within one hour of
giving birth, we can be wrong as many times as we are
right.

In the sheep business, which is unlike the cattle business in one respect, a rancher is always trying to predict if a ewe is going to have twins.

Personally, after years in the business, I'm still learning, still guessing, and still hoping that someone will come along and fill me in on the vital signs. I even find it difficult to predict if a ewe will bear another lamb after the first one is born. My percentage of good guesses has risen in the last few years, but I can still "goof," and badly.

There are certain broken umbilical cords which dangle outside the vagina after the birth. They vary slightly if the ewe has completed lambing, or if there is another lamb still tucked away in the uterus. They vary, also, if the first lamb born was an identical twin. Of course, there is always the possibility she will have triplets, and then all prognoses will be shot down.

SOME people have compared the human birth to that of a lamb probably because the two infants are similar in size. I've never witnessed the former, so I can't say.

I have, though, witnessed thousands of lambs hit the ground and I most certainly can't imagine human babies doing the same. Nor can I imagine a young girl giving birth to a 14-pound young one, but I have seen 110-pound yearling ewes get the job done.

Yearlings usually don't breed and most sheepmen don't even expose them to a ram. I do, but then I feed the hell out of them. For a yearling ewe to breed, she must weigh at least 90 pounds, be seven months old and on the gain. Even then, on an average, only about 50 per cent of the yearling flock will conceive.

It is quite a task for yearlings to reproduce since they are only babies themselves—just weaned and still growing. In the spring after they have lambed, they more often look like an eight-year-old "pelter" ewe.

Since it was only a while ago that the little yearlings were playing in bunches and nursing their mothers, it is understandable that the first instincts of motherhood should be very confusing to them.

When the young mothers taste their offspring for the first time, their motherhood emotions run rampant; they just don't quite understand that their babies are searching for the same "thing" they themselves gave up only five months ago. I've seen a yearling's newborn, in his efforts to reach the tit, take the yearling one quarter of a mile across the field. But, after much blatting and circling, the little ewes will get their ends straightened out and become very devoted mothers.

It is unusual—but it happens to a couple of my lambs every year—that when the young mother becomes so excited from being nursed for the first time, she'll bite the tail off her lamb and sometime his testicles. (I've been told that this "practice" among deer and antelope accounts for the "staggy" males hunters shoot occasionally. Sounds reasonable).

T HE "drop band" is well named. This is exactly
what happens—the lambs are dropped to earth,
and the ewes yet to lamb are referred to as the "drop
band."

A ewe, after her initial struggle with the forehead, will
have little trouble with the birth up to the lamb's hips.
At this point, she has very little left to push on; so, instead of lying on the ground exerting futile pressure on
the lamb's tail and hindlegs, she just simply stands up
and lets gravity pull the lamb the rest of the way out.

Therefore, most lambs arrive on this earth nose first.
This might even be Nature's little contrivance for break-
ing the membrane enveloping the lamb's nostrils, as
well as forcing his first gasp as the little fellow goes
"kerplunk."

(Human babies get spanked and little lambs get dive-bombed. My mother never told me, but I doubt very much if I were "dropped" into this world. It might have been a good idea.)

Occasionally, a lamb will hip-lock, and the force of gravity will be insufficient to complete the birth. But this is really no problem for an old ewe; after a few good spins, the lamb will come flying out and, again, the poor little thing goes "kerplunk."

Spinning the lamb out.

There are times when the lamb will be hip-locked for several minutes. The initial crack-the-whip spins by the mother have by this time, though, forced enough air into the lamb's lungs so he can let out a healthy blat. The blat will inspire another surge of maternal instinct in the old ewe, and she will spin at a more accelerated pace in her effort to reach her young, dangling out there behind her. And Nature, though a little late, has come through with another birth.

A ewe will expell her afterbirth, usually within 30 or 60 minutes after she has given birth. If she doesn't, it means that another lamb is to be born, or is hung up, or she is having other problems.

19

Frequently, though, the afterbirth will hang up temporarily. It then becomes a foreign object, dangling far enough from the vagina to tickle the ewe on her hind legs. The ewe, since she knows the afterbirth isn't another lamb, but still doesn't understand its presence, will get "goosed," and start spinning and running in an effort to rid herself of this unexplained "thing.".

This scene can sometimes turn into a little rodeo, complete with bucks, gallops, and sprints. I have seen a ewe buck and run for over a mile, sometimes bellering and blatting at every fourth leap. In time, though, she'll manage to rid herself of the afterbirth only to face another traumatic period of searching for her newborn who has been wandering from ewe to ewe in search of his rightful mother. If she is an older ewe who has had experience with lost babies, and if her lamb is a single, she'll probably locate it without too much trouble. But if she has given birth to twins, there is bound to be a mixup—not only for the confused mother, but for the confused rancher as well.

20

Wombs and Other
Pieces of Anatomy

*The simple lines
of labor.*

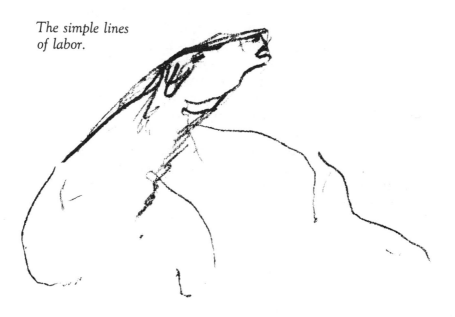

OCCASIONALLY, in every two hundred births or
so, a ewe will have a prolapse of the uterus, or
as we say in the business: "She threw her womb." In
other words, the entire womb turns inside out and
hangs from the vulva all the way to the ground.

This is a scarey sight, since the animal appears to have
lost all her "innards," but the situation is really not as
serious as the first sight of such a ewe might suggest.
The ewe's life can be saved even if she has gone 10 or
12 hours unattended. (I have, though, seen "dudes"

21

almost faint at the sight of this large dangling bag.) Frequently in such cases, the uterus has been dragged for hours across the ground, and it is a filthy mess.

When a cow has a prolapse, the problem is more serious; not because there is a better chance of infection, but because of the size of the animal. In both instances, the rancher must, first, unfasten the placenta (a sort of an unbuttoning procedure) from the walls of the uterus. This can be sort of a confusing and delicate undertaking, because it is difficult to discern where the placenta begins and where the uterus leaves off, and a pull or a rip in the wrong place leaves one with a full-size hemorrhage on his hands.

After the placenta has been removed and the uterus washed with some good old mild soap, the
uterus has to be reinserted
through the
vulva

into its chamber in front of the pelvic bone. With a cow, this can become a very difficult task, considering that her womb weighs approximately 30 pounds, and that this 1000-pound animal is exerting all her force to keep it out. So if the cow has had a complete prolapse, it is almost impossible to replace her womb without the assistance of a "vet" who has available anaesthetics to paralyze her hind-quarters.

A sheepman, however, cannot call in a vet when he has a ewe with a prolapsed uterus because the professional services would cost more than the sheep is worth. There is really no need to anyway, since a mature ewe weighs only 150 pounds. One man is able to hold the ewe up by her hindlegs, which inhibits her convulsive pushes while another man (my wife, in some cases), with the help of gravity, simply pushes the uterus back and fills the cavity with cold well water.

After the animal's uterus has been relocated, it is necessary to sew up the vulva because her involuntary convulsive pushes will force the womb right back out into daylight. Even then, a cow—and sometimes even a ewe—will exert such a force that the stitches will be ripped out. I have seen many techniques employed to hold the uterus in place: everything from sewed-in beer bottles to sharpened willow sticks inserted across the vulva and laced together with leather shoe laces.

My cold-well-water method of retaining the uterus, which also inhibits the sheep's involuntary contractions, seems to work better than anything else I've tried. This technique would probably work with a cow, except she is such a large animal that it is impossible to raise her by her hind legs, even with the help of a hydraulic stacker.

I have compared notes with obstetricians and, surprisingly, discovered that some obstetric techniques don't differ that much from some of the methods we use in delivering and caring for mother ewes. I doubt, though, that any doctor has employed my cold-water method. (It would be a problem positioning the patient, I suppose.)

We, as ranchers, can afford to have a sense of humor

in the presence of pain and misery, even death. God, if we couldn't, we could never survive the cruelties of nature. There are millions of peasants, not unlike myself, around the world who care for millions and millions of animals. We are professional herdsmen and we administer bottles and cases of medicines—all the way from flea powders to complex antibiotics—yet we are not allowed to administer the simple anaesthetics that would relieve so much pain in so many beasts.

If some of you had to witness what we are obliged to inflict on an animal, you would probably collapse in your tracks.

A little lamb will moan and flinch for about five minutes from the pain of a rubber castrating band. I know of no other time that a sheep will utter an exclamation of pain. They will, however, cry out in fear and confusion. This sound, sort of a squeaky blat, is similar to the cry of a captured rabbit, goat, fawn, and several other animals. It is, in fact, imitated on a reed by hunters to attract predators, and even deer who will come in defense of their young.

24

I wish this characteristic of sheep were not so. We have no way of telling, exactly, how much pain we are inflicting on an animal. We don't know how much they can endure; we can only relate their sensitivity to human pain. If this is true—and I hope it isn't—then I'm guilty of being the cruelest of mammals.

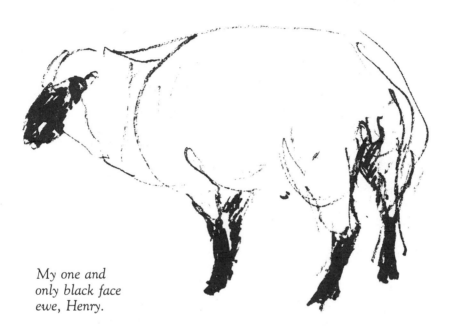

My one and only black face ewe, Henry.

MOST animals eat their afterbirth, and sheep are no exception. But, unlike an old cow who will gobble up every morsel, a ewe will only nibble at it. Sheep are very particular eaters; so, if the afterbirth falls on clean grass, the ewe will eat a much larger portion of it, than if, for instance, it falls in a dirty corral. There, she'll probably not even smell it.

There are theories as to what provokes animals to eat their afterbirth: some will suggest it is nature's way of concealing the evidence of birth, while others contend the placenta contains medicinal qualities. I certainly don't rightly know; and I well imagine the sheep business will continue its erratic course, regardless of

25

whether an old ewe is attracted to this particular hors
d'oeuvre or not.'

A ewe who is about to lamb will usually have
her first pain about one hour before the blessed
event, but sometimes as much as twelve hours in advance. She will become very nervous, start making
motherly noises, paw the ground, and turn in small
circles. If she is out in the pasture with other sheep, she
will separate from the other ewes and more than likely
isolate herself in a corner of the field. The same
maneuver will take place in a corral, but in a more confined way.

If the prospective mother is a good, healthy, older ewe
with many lambs to her credit, she, no doubt, will
become a "granny"—and a damned nuisance in the
"drop" band.

With nature's first signal of an approaching birth, a
"granny" will mother any newborn lamb she can find,
especially those that are still wet—to the distress of all
the other ewes and the rancher as well. Sheep are very
gregarious, non-aggressive animals and seldom fight
among each other, except in protection of their offspring. So, often, in the efforts of the mother ewes to

claim possession of their newborn, the lambs will get
confused, strayed, and sometimes orphaned.

Most of the mixups and confusion at lambing time
come at night; therefore, a good "nightman" when he
works the "drop" band will listen for the very
characteristic throaty blat which identifies the
"grannies" and "jug" them (pen them separately from
the other ewes).

There isn't a "lamblicker" (member of a lambing crew)
who hasn't cursed the bother created by a "granny"; but
when all is said and done, they are a sheepman's best
ewes. We can thank God, though, that not every ewe is
endowed with this affluence of motherly emotions, or
we would be forever straightening out mother and lamb
pairs.

Often I have watched three old "grannies" lamb
together in a corner of the field—all, of course, giving
birth to twins. In my early days when I understood less
about sheep than I do now, I would try to straighten

out mixups. Frankly, I only added to the confusion.

I had to learn to leave them alone. If the weather was nice—and if one of the old "grannies" didn't happen to have triplets—they would sort out their lambs through the maze of 16 combinations or so, nurse them, and lead them to a quieter part of the pasture. If the weather was bad, where it became necessary to haul the ewes and lambs into shelter, I would always end up with one or two orphans, since the chain of smell and taste that attached the ewe to her lambs would be disrupted.

An old ewe might, to the "dudes" and other haters of sheep, appear to be a stupid animal. Believe me, she is not. She knows exactly how many lambs she gave birth to and what they smell like. A ewe's sense of smell and the emotions odors provoke in them is one of nature's finest forms of intelligence given to "dumb" animals. What we as humans fail to appreciate, since our "smellers" are so deficient, is that almost all animals depend on their sense of smell, more than any other sense, to guide them through life. (A coyote, for instance, has a nose like radar; he can detect from a mile away an odor that humans can't smell from a few feet away).

It is only after a ewe's lambs are two or three weeks old that she starts identifying her young by their blat and by sight. Even then, when a mother ewe calls her lambs to nurse, she'll reassure herself of their identity by smelling under their tails.

Births...Births...Births

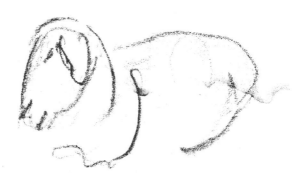

THE day was warm and sunny and a light breeze blew from the southwest—a Chinook wind, if it had been winter. But it wasn't. It was spring, and the odors, sounds and motions of spring followed in the wind. Even the lambs took part. They had just finished playing and they were either hunting for their mothers or lying down to sleep. Occasionally, one would jump high in the air, the spirit of play still with him.

As I walked among them I could recognize certain individuals or pairs—some by their head or body, others by the blue or red chalk marks I had put on their backs to identify them at lambing time. With my foot I nudged a big single with a large red cross on his rump. He never woke up—his sleep was so sound.

"Silly little lamb," I thought, "what an easy prey you would make for a coyote, or even a slow-moving badger."

The memories of this year's lambing skipped through my mind, hardly leaving a ripple. There had been so many experiences, now diluted by the memories of other years. But I did recall this lamb—by the red cross, probably.

I had first noticed his mother in a corner of the lot, all humped up and straining to give birth. When I returned one half hour later, she was still straining and

29

her water had not yet passed.

When I first went into the ewe, I thought it was a case where the cervix hadn't dilated. It wasn't. I was able to poke my finger past the cervix and feel the nose of the lamb; apparently it was just a simple case of a 90 degree twist of the womb.

Actually, the technique in righting a twisted womb is quite simple. I insert my arm as far as I can into the vagina, grab on to whatever I can grip, and let someone spin the ewe. To try to turn a 25 pound sack inside an old ewe with a simple twist of the wrist is next to impossible. (An obstetrician once told me that he turns little babies the same way).

The lamb's skin under the red cross twitched. "Making room for the new cells growing in his body," I mused. "And I guess he'll never know how close he came to being heaped on the dead-lamb pile."

B IRTHS...births...births....I have seen thousands of
them, not only in sheep, but in cattle, horses,
pigs, dogs, cats, rabbits and mice. Once, I almost caught
a skunk at it.

It is so common; yet, I'm drawn to this phenomena
with the same wonderment I had when I was a boy.
When it is right, it is so simple. When it is wrong, it is
nature's cruelest method of paralleling birth with pain
and death.

The lamb's little nose, along with his two front feet, is
the first part of his anatomy to appear in the outside
world. If he doesn't begin his arrival in this order, there
is trouble ahead.

A ewe's pelvic cavity is only so large. (I have never
understood why nature designed it with such small
tolerances.) If it is too small to let both the feet and
head pass at the same time, one leg will be forced back
into the womb; again, if it is still too small, both legs
will be forced back. The mother ewe is now unable to
complete the birth—at least in the time frame for life to
continue in her offspring—since the lamb's shoulders are
too large to be forced past the pelvic opening by the
force the ewe can exert.

This syndrome is the most common lambing problem
we have. Obviously, in such cases, the lamb will have to
be pulled or it will die, as well as the mother. The
technique of pulling the lamb is very simple. The ewe
has to be caught and turned on her side; next, depending if one or two legs are stuck behind the pelvic opening—because it is often possible to pull the lamb by one
leg and his head—it is necessary to push the head back
into the uterus. Now, by holding on to the lamb's jaw
with two fingers and clasping the feet with the remain-
ing fingers and thumb, one starts pulling, taking advan-
tage of whatever pushes the mother ewe might exert,
since, after all, the lamb puller just doesn't have that
good a grip. Above all, patience is the order of the moment.

As soon as the feet and nose have been oriented into
the birth canal and progressed far enough to the outside

so one can get a firm hold on a leg, one pulls the leg out so the shoulder is past the pelvic opening. At this point, by manipulating the legs and forcing the vulva over the lamb's forehead, the puller can pop the lamb right out.

I tried to sneak up on the young ewe and hook her by a hind leg, but I missed on my first pass, and the frightened animal took off at full gallop across the field. The neck and head of the lamb she was trying to birth dangled from her vagina; it bounced and whipped as she ran. Next, I tried to chase her into a fence corner, but again she escaped me. Finally, after a chase of over one half mile, I managed to corner the ewe in a corral.

Even from a distance of one hundred feet, I could see that the lamb's tongue was protruding and that his head was dry and swollen, almost twice its normal size. The ewe, no doubt, had been trying to give birth for several hours.

I could only guess whether the lamb was still alive; God, after all that jostling, it would be wonder if his neck wasn't broken.

I managed to pull the lamb—as I had managed others

All sheepmen have their own technique of catching a ewe, but really nothing beats a long hook, a good wind, and 9.3 speed.

in the past—by one leg, and with a force sufficient, one would think, to tear his little body to pieces.

I pumped his left leg, and blew in his mouth for a minute or so, until he was able to breathe on his own; his head was so swollen, he could barely lift it or open his eyes. I managed to squirt some of his mother's milk past his swollen tongue and massage it down his throat. This was by far the best medicine I could give him.

The poor little lamb (or I should say, the great big single) lived. Oh yes, for days I had to help him nurse, but after four days the swelling receded, and he was on his own. For two weeks, he had problems keeping up with his mother and was unable to play "run-across-the-pasture" with the other lambs. But by the third week,

If you were loaded down with 24 pounds of triplets,
you'd probably look like this
and feel much worse.

though unable to play "flanker," he did "sub" for the "tailback" from time to time.

Recently, a little "dude" girl asked me if I used soap as an antiseptic and lubricant when I pulled a lamb. (She had just acquired a few head of ewes and was very apprehensive about lambing them). Well, there is very little time for such preparations and no need, really, since the natural lubricants and antibiotics of the mother are sufficient. To tell the truth, since little lambs are so slippery, there are many times I would have given a day's wages for a handful of rosin.

My wife, working her shift during lambing, once pulled a big single who was coming hind end first by his tail. This might be a convenient handle but it is not an advisable way to deliver a lamb if it is at all possible to poke him back into the womb and turn him around. This lamb lived, but he did have a broken tail.

35

Oh, how many times I've been "up to my elbows" in lambing. I wonder if my old ewes appreciate my small hands and long, slim arms. I have known a lot of "big handed" sheepmen, and I have often been curious as to how they make out at lambing time. Apparently, most of them do make out; but, my God, what stresses they must inflict on those poor old ewes. Anyway, I do know a couple of my neighbors who went into the cattle business because of their handicap.

Once, I pulled for 15 minutes on the head and legs of a little lamb, but I was unable to get his shoulders past the pelvic opening. Finally, to my embarrassment, I discovered I was pulling on the head of one lamb and the legs of another. This happens quite often; a set of twins will start down the birth canal together and get stuck in the opening.

I have worked on many ewes with this problem, as have all sheepmen. To deliver these lambs, I push the lambs far back into the womb, and then feel around with my fingers to sort out, among the eight extremities, the legs that go with the appropriate body. (Need I explain the difficulties involved if there are triplets all mixed up down in that dark, slippery hole). This isn't easy, since the pressures of the ewe's vagina sap the tone from one's hand and arm muscles to the point where they are partially paralyzed. (In a cow the pressures are four times what they are in a sheep—imagine!) It is sometimes difficult to feel the difference between the front legs and the hind legs. Often I have had to orient myself by the lamb's tail, and even it will sometimes feel much like another leg.

But, in time, after switching arms several times and with the help of a patience I have had to acquire over the years, I have always managed to clamp my hand around the lamb's front feet and neck, and then by merely holding on, I would let the ewe give birth to both her lamb and my hand.

The second lamb is usually much easier to deliver since by this time the birth trail has been well blazed.

Sea of ears.

THE "dudes" in their big cars and campers
come up the country roads, especially on Sunday. Often they stop—either my sheep have blocked the
road, or just out of curiosity, they'll watch the mothers
with their newborns or a ewe giving birth. None of
them have ever left the comfort of their packaged environment to walk across the field and talk to me.
Maybe they are shy or maybe my grisled countenance

would scare a rattlesnake toward his hole. But, after all, we do speak approximately the same language.

Occasionally, I have overheard pieces of their dialogue: "Mommy, what's that thing sticking out of that sheep?" "Bobby, you just don't look at that." The car door would slam and the "dude" family would drive off.

The poor kid. He, no doubt, was pulled into his hamburger-ketchup society on the end of the doctor's tongs, to the nauseating smell of anaesthetics and the muffled screams of his mother. He never even got to nurse on a warm tit or taste the sweet syrup of the first milk. His life was a synthetic existence from the start—homogenized, plasticized, and pureed. He never was allowed to lick the earth, chew on a blade of grass, or even take a pee in the bush.

Again, the poor kid.

I have never seen the lamb I could reach that I couldn't pull; true, some of them had a lame shoulder or a stiff neck for several days, but they did live.

About the only times I have been unable to deliver a lamb was when the ewe's cervix didn't dilate. The alternative then was "to put her out of her misery."

The poor creature—if she had been an expensive animal, such as a cow, I could then have afforded a veterinarian to perform a ceasarian, but since the "vets" services would have cost more than the ewe was worth, a .22 bullet was the economical answer.

What is the price of sentiment? Has the profit motive so saturated philosophies that I can't purchase a life for the only purpose of seeing it continue to live? Are these the accrued calluses of my occupation? I don't dare answer these questions or I would have to become a dirt farmer.

Lambs...Lambs...Lambs

LAMBS...Lambs...Lambs...that is what it is all about: first, lives to be saved, then to be wasted. A paradox for a conscious carnivore—a natural procedure for the insensitive.

I have so many memories of cold, miserable little lambs with stiff, clammy bodies—some so near death I had to hold a cigarette paper to their mouths to see if they were breathing. I have carried armloads of them into the house and warmed them by submerging them in basins of hot water. I have fed them for hours, drop by drop, before I could discern a slight movement in their prostrate bodies.

What has amazed me is how lifeless a lamb can appear and still be revived.

A lot of these lambs will become "bums." Since they were separated from their mothers for hours and washed of their identifying odors, their mothers will refuse to claim them; or, at most, claim only one of them if they were twins.

"Bums" is something of a misnomer, since it refers to orphan lambs. The real "bums" are to be found in every band. They can be readily identified by their dirty heads and their somewhat decrepit appearance. They are lambs who lost their mother when they were two or three weeks old, after they were old enough to fend for themselves.

The poor little fellows. They are obliged to steal their milk supply from the back door from any ewe who is insensitive to being nursed from the rear. They don't dare expose themselves in any normal nursing position to a ewe, other-wise they would be kicked off. So, with a talent invented by necessity, they sneak up behind a ewe while she is nurs-ing her proper lamb and nurse the other tit with the rapidity, I might add, of an air hammer. This accounts for the "bums" dirty, brown head: they have manured entrances to their dining place.

These lean, hungry lambs, always occupied in hunting down another meal, very seldom play with the other lambs or take part in being a sheep in the normal sense. They usually hang by themselves and in general are afraid of the society of sheep. (If one should desire to pursue it, they afford a study in a loveless life.)

42

The other "bums," those orphaned at a day old or so and raised by man, are a different lot. They have never known a mother sheep, and like most young animals, identify with the first thing they see move—later on, that which feeds them.

These farm-yard "bums," unlike their counterpart out in the band, are not really unhappy. They have themselves for company and the other farm animals—cats, dogs, calves, farm kids and the like—to play with. Even though their mother is nothing more than a cold rubber nipple and a bucket of cow's milk, they accept their circumstances as normal. (A study, I suppose, on the relativity of a way of life.)

There are very few old farm or ranch families who haven't raised a bunch of "bums." It is not so common now, since most farmers have been forced to quit milking cows; and the decline in the sheep population has made "bums" difficult to obtain. A few are raised with milk replacers, but only as a hobby for a kid, since the cost of synthetic milk prohibits this practice on an economic basis.

In times past, when it was routine in lambing the big bands to raise only one lamb to a ewe, there were many

"bums" to be had, since the weaker lamb in all twin births was either "knocked in the head" or given away. I have known farm women who have raised as many as 50 or 60 "bums" in a season. Sometimes, this—along with their cream check—was their only income for the year. I don't doubt for a minute that "bums" have been the difference for some farm families in "making it" or not "making it."

For every "bum" raised, there is one who didn't make it. The survival percentage is probably that low since they are usually the weaker lambs, and the change from the ewe's milk to the weaker cow's milk or milk replacer is too difficult for them. Also, if they never had the first milk from their mother to set their sensitive digestive system in order, they have almost no chance of surviving.

These little orphans have to be kept very warm and comfortable for the first month of their lives and fed all they want to eat. Since they are unlike little humans who have very little rapport with their instincts, they will eat when they are hungry and sleep when they are tired.

Anyway, after the "bums" get going, they become vigorous little nuisances around the ranch: small enough

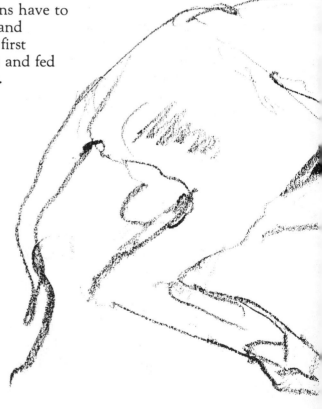

to crawl through most fences, tame enough not to fear
other animals, and knowledgeable enough to know that
humans are the source of their food supply. If they are
not fenced away from the ranch house, or if the ranch
house is not fenced away from them, they are very apt
to be found sneaking
through the kitchen
door or eating
the dog food
on the
back
porch.

I have no doubt that the lamb that followed Mary to school one day was a "bum." Sheep have a "follow" instinct—part of their gregarious behavior—and "bums," who are always afraid of being isolated, will follow most anything. I have had them follow me around the field when I was driving a tractor, sometimes for hours. They very often take up company with the milk cows, the saddle horse, and even the sheep dogs.

In the fall of the year after the "bums" have been weaned from milk, they have to weaned from the ranch. This sometimes is a problem. These little orphans are not even sure they are sheep since they have had their lives so influenced by man. I have hauled them in a pickup out to the pasture and put them with the band, only to discover when I was half-way back to the ranch, that if I didn't hurry, they would beat me home. Sometimes I had to repeat this maneuver several times—hiding from them on occasions—before they learned to accept sheep as one of their own kind. (A statement, if you wish, on the age-old "B.S." of environment versus heredity.)

I have a six-year-old ewe out in the band. I call her "flopears" since, for some reason or other, her ears are not rigid as sheep ears normally are. She was raised as a "bum" and to this day, she has not forgotten her "upbringing." All I have to do, if I want to bring the band in, is to rattle a grain bucket and holler, "Flopears." She will come to me from over a half mile away, bringing the rest of the band with her. Needless to say, she is worth any two sheep dogs. When I go out among the sheep, I try to remember to carry a small portion of grain with me to feed her. This old pet ewe knows this very well, and in case I forget to feed her, she'll keep nudging me and searching my pockets until I do. In a couple of years she will be too old to come galloping over the hills, her ears bouncing with every stride. Simply said: I'll miss her.

Thousands of years ago, when man first domesticated the sheep species, it didn't take him long to discover

that an old ewe would mother a foster lamb, providing
it carried the skin of her own lamb. The practice
through the ages of "grafting" lambs still continues,
despite our "technological" answers to all ancient ways
of doing things; and it has offered motherhood to many
an old ewe and a normal life to a multitude of "bums."
Anyone visiting a sheep outfit today is sure to find in
the corner of the corral the bodies of skinned lambs and
in the lambing shed, live lambs
with strange overcoats,
particularly after
a storm

SINCE ewes
identify their
young by odor and
not by sight, it is
necessary to skin
the dead lamb and
from the pelt make an
overcoat for the lamb to
be "grafted." This is the usual manner. There are other
ways such as saturating the foster lamb with mother's
milk, rubbing him in her afterbirth, or pouring kerosene
on the ewe's nose to inhibit her ability to smell. (In the

last few years the spray-can people have come on the market with "Mother-up." In the sheep society the old ewes are still laughing over this one. It doesn't work.)

Anyway, if none of these tactics work, a rancher can force a ewe to accept a lamb by penning the pair and holding the ewe while the lamb nurses. After this procedure has been repeated for about three days, or until the scent of the ewe's milk is present in the lamb's feces, the ewe will claim the foster lamb as her own. Frankly, many ewes are difficult to fool; it all depends on her age and how long her proper lamb had nursed before it died.

Seventy percent of my ewes have twins and seven percent of them have triplets. In fact, I'm sort of cursed of having such a prolific band, since one of each set of triplets, and even an occasional twin, has to be taken from his mother and found another parent.

Hardly a day passes during lambing time when I won't be out among the drop band with a little orphan lamb under my arm waiting for a ewe to start lambing so I can "graft" my charge to another ewe. The problem here is always the same: is the ewe who is about to give birth going to have a single or not? If she isn't (and she usually isn't), I have wasted my time. Needless to say, there have been many days when I've wandered around all day long, unsuccessful in finding a new mother for my little "bum."

Eventually, I'll find a potential mother. I can recognize a ewe who in all probability will have a single; she will usually be a younger ewe and in better condition since she is only carrying a single fetus, than the average ewe. I wait until the ewe has gone through the preliminaries of giving birth and until the lamb's feet are visible. Then, with the skill of an old mountain man, I sneak—sometimes crawl—up on her blind side, catch her by a hind leg, and hold her to the ground. I place the little "bum" directly beneath the ewe's vagina and then reach in and pull the ewe's lamb so it, and all the other "stuffs" of birth, fall on the "bum." I wallow him in the afterbirth until he is completely wet; this is very necessary since a wise old ewe most certainly isn't going to accept a dry lamb that supposedly just came from her womb. (It is advisable to wet the "bums," if at all possible beforehand. Often, I've done this by submerging them in the water trough, in mud puddles, and even in snow banks.)

After I have run my hand back into the ewe to make sure she isn't going to give birth to another lamb, I squirt a couple swallows of the mother's milk in each of the lambs' mouths and a little under the "bum's" tail. Next I tie the lambs together with a piece of twine and place them under the ewe's nose.

As soon as the ewe has smelled and tasted both of the lambs, I get her to her feet and then watch her very closely for about ten minutes to see if she makes any effort to bunt off the "graft." If she lets the "graft" nurse, I know that my efforts to fool her have been successful.

Sheep, like most animals, will identify more readily with their newborn at the place of birth, so, for this reason I leave the ewe with her made-up twins alone for about an hour before I take the trio to the shed and pen them. It is quite necessary to pen them together for at least three or four days, so the smaller "graft" can gain enough vigor to keep up with his larger foster-brother in the clamor over the tits.

Every year I graft off about 15 "bums" in this manner. Most of them are successful, and about the only problem I have, is that when the lambs reach the age of three or four weeks, the ewe's proper lamb has so grown in size that he dominates both tits, leaving the poor little "graft" only a stripper source of milk. But the "bum," even if he dies, will have enjoyed a few weeks activity of being a normal lamb.

The Little Non-gourmet

THE sheep band was bunched on the mountain side in an unnatural group. It was unusual, since most mornings they scatter out to paw for grass, now softened by the new snow. I knew what was wrong: it was only a question of where, who, and how many. As I started up the mountain, I saw the fox scamper over the ridge and disappear into the brush coulee. So I knew the "who".

A few weeks before I had had two ewes hamstrung by a fox, and now, obviously, he was back. I didn't have to search long for his victim; I could see the blood spot on the side of the mountain from 300 yards away, and it was not difficult to follow the ewe's bloodstained trail to a nearby brush patch.

The wounded ewe stood with her head down; the skin from her hindquarters had all been torn away and was hanging limp in the snow. Like most "dumb" animals, especially sheep, she uttered no sound: there were no moans, no groans, only a narrowed eye in response to the pain.

With my help, the ewe managed to drag herself to another pasture, isolated from the other sheep. For two days I carried her water and hay, and I did my best to doctor her massive wound. On the third day, the loose skin began to rot and smell, and that evening I turned my mind off—as I'm required to do quite often—and I shot her. I hauled her body to the top of a nearby ridge; there her flesh would feed the magpies and the eagles; there her bones would revitalize a few square feet of earth. There was no chance that the fox would return to eat on her cold body—not with all the warm, live sheep walking around.

Maybe a veterinarian could have saved the ewe's life, but I doubt it. Maybe if I had left the ewe where she

51

had been attacked, the fox would have returned and finished the kill, but I doubt it. A fox is too small to kill a mature ewe in the way of a coyote; they only play at being wolf.

Storms and Other Disasters

THE four foremost enemies of any agricultural
enterprise are the weather, insects, predators,
and markets. A rancher can usually devise some means
to combat the latter three, but the weather is such a for-
midable force that we are at its mercy most of the time.

We can build shelters and listen to weather forecasts,
of course. This we do. But there seems to be, almost
every year, that one storm which has escaped the attention of the meteorologists or the availability of our
shelters—especially in Montana.

In this northern, Rocky Mountain region, the weather
is a paradox, and one must have lived here most of his
life to understand it—which we don't try to do, inciden-
tally—or to appreciate it. I can't imagine myself living,
for instance, under the constant sun of Southern
California. My God, what a bore.

Our climate, east of the Rocky Mountains in Montana—a climate affected from the west by the warm
Chinook winds of the Pacific, from the north by the
arctic fronts, from the southeast by the humid, upslope
conditions coming out of the Gulf of Mexico and the
highs from the desert southwest—is dramatic, severe,
and to say the least, diversified. We can have summer in
winter and winter in summer.

I have seen the weather change in a twelve-hour
period from 40 below zero to 40 above zero. I have seen
the earth baked for weeks on end beneath a desert sun
of 110 degrees, so not even a grasshopper could find a
bite to eat, and drenched under a downpour of sixteen
inches of rain in the month of May. I have battled three
feet of snow and temperatures that never rose above 20
below zero for the entire month of February, and I have
fixed fence in my shirt sleeves and walked among the

53

*Sheared, pregnant sheep
in snow storm.*

blooming crocuses on Lincoln's birthday. When I was a kid, I once went swimming in the creek on the first day of March.

I have also walked knee-deep on the 20th of April among the frozen bodies of hundreds of dead sheep, piled in fence corners in their efforts to escape a drop of four feet of snow.

The Chinook winds which invade Montana's winter weather are more responsible than any other factor in making our weather unique. The word "Chinook" is used to describe these winds, since in the early days of the West, they were thought to originate in the Chinook Indian villages on the West Coast. All I can really explain about the Chinooks is that they are the cool Pacific fronts which are compressed against the west side of the Rockies. The compression causes the air to heat, and it then spills over the mountains as warm, dry winds. They usually come in quite shallow and sometimes their air mass is only a few hundred feet thick. Most of the time the currents blow in about 30 miles per hour, hugging the valleys and pushing the cold air masses to higher alitutudes. But I have watched the Chinooks melt snow high on the mountain tops, while the valleys remained frigid.

It is interesting to observe the Chinook's skirmishes with the massive artic fronts. Although they have never won the "Climatic War," the Chinook currents have won many battles against "General Cold" and have so often given ourselves and our animals a touch of spring in the middle of January and dreams of another season.

> It is cold,
> And the hold
> That winter has
> Will not pass
> Till spring is old.

I wrote this little observation many years ago and, if I remember correctly, a Chinook came in and made me out a liar two days after I had written it.

Although the Chinooks are periodically chased back over the mountains or completely absorbed by the massive cold, their influence does remain, sometimes for only a few hours but usually for a couple of days. Often, however, their patrols against the cold of the north are sufficient to invite the enormous warm highs from the desert southwest—and then we have summer in winter.

This is our weather—unpredictable, to say the least. And, regardless of all the severe conditions we have endured and of all the memories of lost livestock, it takes only two lovely days of Indian Summer in late September—days I cannot describe—to make Montana's climate the most enjoyable one I have ever lived in.

What is nature without contrast? What are days that never change? What is life without anticipation? Urban life, perhaps. May God deliver me from that particular air-conditioned monotony.

Most urban peole are quite astonished to learn that western ranchers leave livestock outside when the temperature has plummeted to 40 below zero. Well, they are cold, of course. I have seen little short-haired Jersey cows almost freeze to death. On the other hand, I have watched a band of sheep with three inches of wool on their backs stand on the lee side of a hill and very unconcernedly chew their cuds and participate in the quiet understanding of being a sheep.

The secret to withstanding the severe cold is a windbreak. The long hair on Hereford and Angus cattle and the wool on sheep, if it is not penetrated by the wind, affords a perfect insulation against frigid conditions. What has always amazed me is why our animals don't more often freeze their feet, ears or udders. Occasionally, they do. But except for the newborn, I have rarely seen it happen. I can only suggest that they must have extra large blood vessels in their extremities.

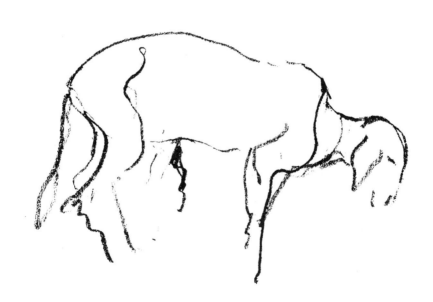

Obviously, we do afford shelter to our animals during severe storm periods if the natural shelters of brush, coulees and woods are not available. But all livestock do much better in their natural environment than in the unsanitary conditions surrounding sheds, barns, and corrals, even if they are a little cold.

No rancher in this section of North America has escaped the ravages of the spring blizzards; these are the storms that can be so devastating to the livestock industry. A Montana rancher has no difficulty, despite the extreme cold and the winter blizzards of December, January, and February, in wintering mature livestock—especially sheep. True, a cold spell in mid-winter can thin down and even weaken the older ewes, but a few warm days in February, when the herds can again move around and paw for a little grass, will return the good life to their bodies.

Freshly sheared sheep humped
up in a cold rain.

A lot of sheepmen have postponed their lambing operation until May to avoid as far as possible the equinox storms in April which are capable of dumping three feet of snow in a 24-hour period. These storms are often joined by winds up to 50 miles per hour, and I have seen grown cattle go down under the pressures of wet, blowing snow.

One of these severe tempests struck eastern Montana a few years ago on the 25th of April. Tens of thousands of ewes and lambs, thousands of calves, all sorts of wildlife, and even mature cows and horses were suffocated in this terrible blizzard. The actual number of

livestock lost in this particular storm—or for that matter, any storm—will never be known, since ranchers are very reluctant to talk of their losses.

The "dude" world is quite unaware from the comforts

of their air-conditioned monotony of what goes on in the country. I suppose they couldn't care less, since their only discomfort from bad weather is a taxi ride downtown instead of driving their own car.

The day after one of these storms, the local newspaper will carry a picture of an electric pole which blew over and an accompanying article on how some community "suffered" for 10 hours without electricity. That's all. No mention of the thousands of dead animals or of the millions of dollars lost to the economy. Oh yes, I almost forgot—there is always a picture of a stranded kitty cat.

Sheep are a contradiction, able to withstand extreme cold and extreme heat. They can survive a winter with little more to eat than sagebrush; they can produce milk from sparse, desert plants, and I have watched a band of sheep turn away from a lush pasture of timothy and clover to lunch on the bitter leaves of chokecherry bushes.

Sheep like it high and dry. Their hoofs will grow long and curl at the ends and their stomachs will become in-fested by worms if they are left too long on low, soft pasture. Moisture, it seems, is their worst enemy. (One

A bloated ewe—victim of the good life.

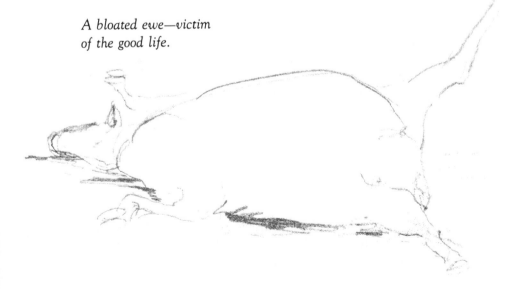

only has to see the misery of a cold, rain-soaked ewe to believe my words.) I have seen little lambs born at 10 below—and despite their frozen feet, tails, and ears—survive. On the other hand, I have watched three-week-old lambs succumb to a cold rain.

Yes, lambing time in Montana is a precarious time for the sheep industry. A sheep rancher can be wiped out by just one storm—in fact, many have been. Therefore, a lot of ranchers have postponed their lambing until May, to avoid the below-zero weather in March and the wet snows in April. But even May lambing is not without its problems.

I would like to explain here in words what is involved in lambing out several hundred ewes when one is hit by a storm, but I may not be able to. I find it difficult because one must experience it to truly understand it.

These are the desperate hours. Our economic survival is tied to the lamb's survival. There is no such thing as an 8 to 5 shift; it is go, go, go, until one can go no longer....It is a fatigue that reaches the last fibers of one's body, and then a rebirth of energy as nature's second wind enables one to continue for a few more hours....It is pickups stuck in the snow, and tractors that won't start....It is dragging bales of hay for hundreds of yards through drifts to feed stranded bunches of sheep....It is watching hay supplies dwindle and listening to weather forecasts that speak of no hope....It is lifting 160 pound wet, slippery ewes into the back of trucks and digging out half-frozen lambs from snow drifts....It is blatting, confused sheep crammed into the garage, chicken coop, granary or any other available shelter....It is a kitchen littered with slimy, chilled lambs and a good wife trying to nurse a flicker of life back into their frigid bodies....It is searching for mother ewes, separated from their babies, and it is skinning cold dead lambs in order to graft an orphan to a lambless mother.

But above all, it is the mounting pile of dead lambs in the corner of the corral and the frozen afterbirths that only a few hours before had enveloped the warm life of the unborn.

The vague lines
of death.

And it is measuring snow drifts and comparing this storm to others of years past....It is comments with your neighbor: "Hell, it coulda been worse—lost 40 head of yearling ewes in the one in '55"....It is counting your few blessings and ignoring your losses.

But storms, like all living things born of this world, must die. And so the snow melts, giving its life to the grass; and the grass, its life to the mother ewe; and the ewe, her life to the lamb. The memories of a storm are brief—a few days of warm spring weather and the sight of a ewe giving birth to a pair of bouncing twins makes us again appreciate the value of our way of life.

FOR every device nature invented to destroy life, she created two other means to continue it. She did so with the first milk. It is liquid life.

Although ingenious, scientific man has imitated the first milk (colostrum), he in no way has recreated it—and for my part, he never will. True, he can synthesize its calciums, phosphates, trace mineral, its antibiotics, antibodies, proteins and sugars. But all his solutions fall short of that ingredient which will dry off a lamb, shrivel his umbilical cord within minutes, and enable him to resist winter weather when he is only a few hours old.

The first milk is often more important than shelter. I have seen new-born lambs with their little bellies full of the first milk of their mother, lie out in the field on a cold, spring day, and yawn back at the weather—while their cousins, weeks older and no longer getting colostrum, chill and eventually die of pneumonia.

One practice for ranchers in times past when lambing

out the larger bands in areas where help was scarce and shelter non-existent was to catch every ewe immediately after she dropped her lamb and squirt three or four swallows of milk into the lamb's mouth. This technique would certainly not save the life of every lamb, but it would keep some of them alive long enough to find the tit on their own, or until the storm broke. However, I might add, it was not unusual in lambing out he big bands during a wet snow storm to truck out a pickup load of dead lambs every morning.

It has always been a toss-up for a rancher to decide whether or not to lamb his ewes in the convenient confinement of his corrals and sheds, where an outbreak of scours or mastitis can contribute to as many deaths as those suffered by lambs on a clean pasture but subject to radical changes in the weather. Anymore, most ranchers use both practices, depending on weather forecasts.

When all is said and done, weather is our friend and our enemy. The heavy, wet snows which take the lives of thousands of young livestock are necessary for the bounties of grass and water that continue the lives of those that do survive.

The Forgotten Ones

I cannot be so negligent as to not offer a few paragraphs of observation on the male side of the sheep business—the bucks. They, too, do their bit, however brief and non-lingering.

I am sure from my male point of view that bucks (rams) have the "life of Riley." They get to lie around all spring and summer, enjoying only male company, nibbling at the choicest pastures, drinking from the best water holes, loitering in the best shade, and just doing nothing. Oh, occasionally, a genetic memory will inspire them to rehearse for battle, but their little bunt-head practice sessions always peter out, and no one gets hurt and nothing is accomplished.

Like all cleft-footed animals, the bucks stay as far away from female company during the off-breeding season as the fences will permit. I have often watched a bunch of bucks chewing their cuds under a shade tree in the middle of summer and wondered about the thoughts that occupied their minds. At this time of the year, with

A Rambouillet buck.

the old breeding season seven months behind them and the new season four months away, do they think about sex? Do they make plans for it? Do they anticipate in any way their one month of glory? I would like to think so.

There are a couple of species of sheep that will breed the year around. But the common breeds of Rambouillet, Columbia and Targhee bucks will not get inspired until after the month of August. From this

month on, they have to be corralled or the rancher will be lambing out his ewes during the blizzards of January. In fact, many ranchers have lambed out at least a part of their band during this month. This hasn't happened to me yet, but if even one buck escapes the corral, he is quite capable of breeding thirty ewes before morning. This might suggest why nature has seen fit to "rest" the male sheep for several months. All *Homo sapiens* should take note of these natural facts: distance and time makes hearts grow fonder and also produce bounties of active sperm.

71

Finally, after months of rest and many mock battles, the bucks are turned in with the ewes. For the first hour or so there is a wild scramble to take part in nature's way, but then the bucks settle down and—unlike the deer, for example, who guard their harems with greed—share their good fortune of the moment.

Oh sure, there will be ancient instincts aroused from time to time and a few heads will collide, but all in all the bucks have a general attitude: "Well, if I get there first—good. If not—there is always another one around the bend."

The proof of what I have just said is that ewes very often give birth to twin lambs, sired by different fathers. And the ewe? She certainly has the right to make the most of her one and only romantic night of the year.

"THE sheep business is a good business. It's the only one where one gets three crops a year: the lambs, the wool, and the pelts."

This old western saying no longer runs true, since, anymore pelts bring only about "four bits," and ranchers don't even bother to skin a dead sheep.

There was a time, 30 or 40 years ago, when a man trying to get into the ranching business could buy a band of old ewes in the Fall for one or two dollars per head. In all probability, 50% of them would die before spring; but the rancher was still in business, since a pelt could be sold for $1.50 and many of the ewes that survived would have twins. There are thousands of farmers, ranchers, and homesteaders who arrived in the sheep business in this manner. Today, of course, none of them will admit to their bleak hours of skinning dead ewes or of trying to get "old pelters" to accept their offspring, and I can count scores of ranchers who completely lost their sense of humor as a result of this experience.

Ewes are excellent mothers, providing they are young, healthy and have a full udder of milk. It seems that the tension in the ewe's udder is nature's most provocative way of instilling motherhood in all animals, and if a band of ewes lack milk, either due to a shortage of feed

or because of old age, the problems at lambing time are quadrupled.

I have seen old ewes give birth, turn and look at their lambs, then without even a feeble blat, walk away and start grazing. It is a pathetic picture: a ewe's last effort, knowing she can no longer produce nourishment for her young, to decide to continue her own life at least.

I have looked at many an old ewe, standing on her last earthly legs, and considered her life's function for man. In her eight years of life, she produced 80 pounds of raw wool (40 pounds, clean), 1,000 pounds of live lamb (400 pounds on the meat counter) and, in doing so, consumed a mixed diet of 12,000 pounds of grass, weeds, brush, hay, and grain. She gave up two of her babies to the weather and one to predators. In all this, I think the weather was the only one who deserved part of her life.

I have always considered old-age nature's "lousiest" way of terminating life. Even I could conceive many alternatives.

The Gourmet Three

I can see the crow in the distance and two magpies fly overhead. There is a strange quietness in the band for this early morning hour.

As I drive up, an old ewe turns to smell her lamb and then stamps her foot in a very characteristic gesture, indicating that she would like to be left alone. A pair of twins scamper over and hurriedly nurse their mother.

The crow tears a piece of warm flesh from the rib cage of a dead lamb—one of three—and then retreats to a fence post some 200 yards away. The magpies dart in for their hors d'oeuvres of eyeballs before they fly off.

A young ewe is blatting and searching among the hundreds of her lambs for offspring, uncertain whether it was her little one who was carried off. The mothers of the three dead lambs are grazing nearby. They don't blat: they have already smelled the death in their babies, and the wastefulness of remorse is not of their nature.

To me the scene is all too familiar—one I have witnessed scores of times. A COYOTE HAS KILLED.

Coyotes are the wisest, cleverest, most intelligent, and suspicious animal on the North American Continent, and a most devastating predator. Volumes could be written about all the tricky exploits attributed to these animals. There are still old-time trappers—of the type who "earned their beans" back in the Twenties and Thirties, trapping coyotes for the fur and bounty—who can relate hundreds of tales of how they were usually outsmarted.

The coyotes welcomed with outstretched jaws the first bands of sheep trailed into the West. Here was a gourmet's delight and the easiest of prey. With the sheep around, they no longer had to fight off a doe antelope for her fawn, or sneak in behind the wolves to gnaw on a buffalo carcass, or try to catch a prairie dog before he made it to his hole. No, they just had to wait until the sheepherder went to sleep and eat their fill.

Most people are unaware of how many coyotes still exist in certain regions of the West, but their numbers run into the thousands. In our two-county area, the predator control agent must eliminate every year a multitude of coyotes to keep their numbers at a constant level. They are rarely seen but the evidence of their kills among lambs is all too evident.

Coyotes, being the gourmets that they are, always kill lambs. They have to be very hard-pressed for food before they'll kill any sheep over a year old.

In the spring of the year, when the lambs are small, the bitch and dog coyote are feeding and caring for a litter of pups, and nothing pleases them more than a convenient band of sheep to prey on.

Their technique of the hunt varies little from year to year, or pair to pair. Sometimes the bitch and dog will hunt as a pair; other times they will hunt individually, often on alternate nights. Unlike the bobcat, who sneaks into the band in the middle of the night and stealthily kills five or six lambs without disturbing the band, the coyotes always take the lamb on the dead run with a bite to the brain. They'll never kill a straggler, only the healthiest and fattest. (I've had an old coyote trapper convince me that a coyote would never kill a jack rabbit if it didn't run.) In the fall of the year when the lambs are fairly well grown, coyotes will kill them with a throat bite. (It is also this time of year when the bitch and dog are teaching their pups how to hunt; subsequently, lamb losses can be substantial.)

It is usually their habit to kill three or four in one night and then choose the most delectable one among the victims. Coyotes will then open the lamb in the flank and first dine—being the gourmets that they are— on the clabbered milk in the lamb's stomach. Next, they'll enjoy a course of warm liver, topped off with a

bite or two of loin or hindquarters before they leave, carrying one of the slaughtered lambs with them. Upon reaching their den, he or she will regurgitate the meal for the pups, saving the whole lamb for tomorrow's dinner.

When a coyote den is located in sheep country, the den site will always be littered with lambs' legs and carcasses. It is my theory that on the nights the bitch hunts alone, she'll simply carry off a lamb without killing others in excess. At least, this is my explanation why lambs vanish from the band.

Coyotes have very strong necks compared to other canines and are capable of carrying, in their jaws, weights in excess of their own body weight. They have been known to carry off a cow's head, and a 15 or 20 pound lamb is no problem at all.

One spring I was losing lambs to a pair of coyotes at the rate of seven or eight per week. We were unable to backtrack them, and a thorough search of their usual denning areas failed to yield clues as to their whereabouts. Finally, with some luck, the government trapper located a den over five miles from my band and killed the dog and all the pups. The killing among my lambs immediately stopped.

As it turned out, this pair, singularly or together, had been crossing a creek, a highway, two woven-wire fences, a county road, a railroad, and another creek to kill from my band, when all the time another band of sheep was grazing within a mile of their den site. Not only that—they had carried the lambs that distance.

Old-time trappers have explained to me that coyotes never hunt in the immediate vicinity of their den. This then may be their technique to divert attention from the location of their pups.

This might illustrate the elusiveness of these animals and why they are at times impossible to trap, difficult to hunt, and just as difficult to poison; why, after all these years since their natural food source of buffalo carcasses, prairie dogs and the like have long disappeared, they are still on the western ranges and getting more numerous every year. (Man exterminated the wolf 70 years ago, but he'll never exterminate the wily coyote as long as the West remains in a semi-primitive state. I hope not—his character gives quality to the prairie, the rough country, and the mountains which are his home—but he must be controlled if for no other reason than to save his species.)

The average urban dweller ("dude" in our country) has no idea of how much effort the ranchers, trappers, hunters, and government control agents have put on the coyote in the last 50 years just to keep their population close to an ecological balance. Now, with the new restrictions on hunting and poisoning coyotes—and as prolific as they are—their numbers could very well triple in the next two years. If this happens, many sheepmen will be forced out of business. The restrictions are not "saving" the coyote.

It is not a pleasant task to destroy animals of any species, but anyone who says that "getters" and 1080 are inhumane has never seen a "gut-shot" coyote, or one after it has suffered for hours in a steel trap; nor has he watched nature destroy an overpopulation of animals or birds by disease or starvation. We, who have lived our lives in the open spaces of the West, have.

The average western rancher knows only too well what can happen to overly-congested livestock in terms of behavior, disease, and internal parasites. He would be the last one to wish to see the extermination of any species—whether it be coyotes, eagles, bobcats, fox, coons, weasels, skunks, mice, rabbits, gophers, woodchucks, moles, porcupines, beaver, etc.

Ranchers have a love for animals—that is why they are ranchers. And since they have lived their lives surrounded by the hundreds of creatures which make up our wildlife, they have more affinity with, for example, the field mouse, and more appreciation of his ecological importance than the "dude" ecologist. Most ranchers whom I know are quite willing to sacrifice a domestic animal now and then to the predators, but not half their herd. But he would also be the first to understand the need to control their density so they can live in rapport with their surroundings.

The ecology of the "Old West" cannot be restored; to do so, we would have to rid the ranges of man and rehabilitate the wolf, the prairie dog, and the buffalo. We must live with what we have, and in the meantime, search for better answers than now exist.

The coyotes, along with the other predators, could almost annihilate the deer and the antelope, the ground nesting birds, and raise havoc among calves. In many areas this is already taking place.

But it will probably come to this before our urban-oriented society will realize that only man can control these wily animals—and that he, man, is also part of the ecological plan—and that the urban food supply as well as ours is involved.

WHILE coyotes attack sheep in a commando style; with the bear the scene is a full-fledged battle ground.

Sheep are very helpless in protecting themselves from this large animal. I consider myself quite fortunate to live 20 miles from bear country, and I, therefore, have never witnessed the slaughter a bear can commit on a band of sheep. It can be a disaster: this I know.

Bears don't even bother with lambs. They are the gourmets who really enjoy a diversified diet, and like man, who will waste
a whole goose just
to taste pate
de fois gras, a
bear will slaughter
seven or eight ewes
in one night just
to sup on their udders.

It is bad enough
to have lambs
killed by smaller
predators, but at
least the ewe has
survived to produce
again. When a bear
gets in a band
and kills only
lactating ewes,
lambs are left
motherless to die
of slow starvation.

Again, thank God, I don't live any closer to bear country. But I suppose—since they, too, are on the increase—they'll again invade this foothill country which was their original habitat.

A coyote kills cleanly and neatly and very seldom just wounds an animal. The golden eagle, though, is just the opposite—it wounds far more animals than it ever kills outright.

An eagle will attack a sheep of any size. When it attacks a lamb, it will descend on its back, driving its talons through the chest cavity. Most of the time, if the lamb is a month old or so, it will escape. I've seen lambs come in, still managing to keep up with the band, with air whistling out holes on both sides of their chest. A day or so later they will die, as one stands helplessly by, unable to doctor them back to health.

When the eagle attacks yearling sheep, it realizes that its talons can't perforate the lungs, so it strikes the eye on the head several times until it manages to puncture the brain. Again, most of the sheep manage to escape which makes no difference to the eagle since the yearling will die eventually from infection, and it can eat on it the following day or week—enjoying (I hope not) its gourmet bits of brain and head skin.

Among bands of sheep in more isolated country where they are not closely watched, an eagle will conveniently perch on the back of a less active, older ewe and simply dine on her rear end while she walks around. As soon as that particular ewe dies, the eagle just flies over and perches on another.

I'm sorry, but I don't appreciate the eagle as a symbol

84

for our country, and I don't even want to write about them.

I like meadowlarks.

A young lamb taloned by an eagle.

More about Coyotes

HERE are some more notes and anecdotes about coyotes I have amassed over the years from talking to trappers. Some I have experienced myself.

...A coyote will never cross a bridge or go through an open gate. He will, however, crawl under the gate if the gate is closed.

...It will avoid crossing a newly constructed fence.

...It loves lamb but will seldom eat on a cold carcass, even if it has killed it itself. Also, it has to be very hungry before it will kill an old ewe or eat on the carcass of one that died.

...Besides being a killer in its own right, it is also a scavenger. In the primitive West, it followed wolves around just to gnaw on the buffalo carcasses the wolves had killed.

...One of its favorite meals is horse flesh—and it doesn't matter whether the meat is two hours or two months old.

...Occasionally it will feed on the remains of a dead coyote.

...It eats berries, fish, eggs, snakes, and all young animals and birds. It will not eat hawks, eagles, magpies, crows, badgers, skunks, weasels, etc.

...It will kill a porcupine by flipping it on its back and disembowling it.

...It will also kill rattlesnakes and eat them. In fact, many trappers use the scent of rotten rattlesnake to attract coyotes to their sets.

...It will unearth steel traps and turn them upside down—almost as if to ask, "Who in the hell are you trying to fool?"

...It has never been known to step on a trap covered only with leaves or grass. Coyote trappers bury their

*A coyote eyeing a
drifted-in sheep.*

traps in at least one-half inch of fine dirt—and then
hope. Some trappers go to such extremes as to set their
traps months in advance of scenting or baiting the set.

...It has the most sensitive nose of all animals. A trapper told me that once he had trailed a coyote who had
suddenly left the trail at right angles; it had walked
over, 50 yards away, and dug out an old sardine can
buried in three feet of snow.

...Many ranchers riding on the range insist a coyote
can smell if you are carrying a gun. At least, I've never
seen one when I had a gun with me.

...They never howl during the denning period.

...Coyotes mate for life and have an average litter of
five or six pups, and under ideal conditions, as many as
nine. They breed in January and February and pup in
April and May. They sometimes mate and breed as
yearlings, but usually as two-year-olds.

...They have been known to den in hollow trees and
culverts, and even under old shacks, but their usual den
site is made from refurnishing an old woodchuck hole or
badger diggings.

...The dog coyote will continue to feed and care for
the pups if the bitch happens to get killed. He also acts

as the sentinel around the den and the vanguard in all hunts. When the bitch and dog travel together, the dog will be out front by 100 to 200 yards.

...It will use diversionary tactics when leaving the den to hunt, but once it has made a kill, it will return to the den on a straight beeline.

...A pair of coyotes will divide their pups as soon as they are big enough to travel into two dens—often, as far as one mile apart. No doubt this is simply another act of self-preservation.

...A bitch has been known to kill lambs as far as 13 miles from her den. She has, also, been known to move her pups in one night, if her den has been disturbed, to a new home 8 miles away.

...A pair of coyotes will abandon their den if it is disturbed by man, leaving their pups to starve; but they'll fight a bobcat or any size or breed of dog in defense of it.

...If a lactating cow or ewe dies on the range, a coyote

Magpies usually have enough restraint to wait until the lamb is unconsious before they dine on hors d'oeuvres of eye balls.

will sever the udder almost with the precision of a surgeon and carry it to its den.

...An old trapper once told me that an antelope always has twin fawns—one for herself and one for the coyotes.

...They always "work" antelope and deer in pairs—one does the decoying while the other dashes in for the fawn.

...Coyotes love to chase matured deer and hamstring them. They sometimes do this in relays and packs of four or five, herding them into a drift of crusted snow. They are too smart to try to outrun an antelope.

...Although coyotes have an inherent fear of the scent of man, they have been known to paw and roll in his excrement.

...My friend the trapper was once trying to catch a wise old dog coyote in a prairie dog town. He had invented a set with which he had had considerable success: he would kill a prairie dog and mount it on a wire stake in a life-like manner at the entrance to the burrow. He then set two traps at a distance of three feet from the bait.

This particular coyote had approached the set on several occasions: it would scratch around until it located the traps and then simply jump over them and steal the bait. Finally the trapper, discouraged after losing four baits and not having another dead prairie dog available, kicked some dirt over the uncovered traps and walked off—not even bothering to re-bait the set. The next morning he had caught the coyote. His explanation of why the old dog walked into the trap was that it had assumed since there wasn't a bait on the stake, there wasn't a trap there either.

This little story proves that even coyotes, like humans, make mistakes—and this is the only way a trapper can catch them.

90

This little story proves that even coyotes, like humans, make mistakes—and this is the only way a trapper can catch them.

The magpies will peck at the sheep's sores and the black birds will peck at their lice.

Thoughts on a Snowy Tuesday

IF I were asked to give only one item of advice to a
young person, it would be to visit a sheep ranch
for one week during lambing time. I know of no other
place where one can observe so many ramifications of
nature in such a short span of time; it is the ideal environment to study the inter-relation of birth, life, and
death—even the philosophy of which might have come
first.

I have no answers to the cruelities of nature on
one hand and all her joys on the other; why
she has devised so many ways to continue life and just
as many ways to destroy it. I often wonder as I watch
nature work if death is nothing more than a means of
filling life with anticipation, and if life is merely a brief
game of hide and seek.

S O with sheep: probably the only mammal who fully comprehends fate.

In our society, where violence is equated with intellect, it has become repulsive for most men to even imagine that any animal can relax in the grip of the inevitable—that it can be so stupid. From my point of view—so intelligent?

I would often kid my friend, the mayor, by telling him that if I managed my sheep the way he managed his "livestock," I would go broke.

He would grin, since he assumed I was being my usual facetious self. He died before I had an opportunity to explain to him how serious I really was. The reason I never purused the subject was that I knew he considered his congested constituents the children of God, and I knew there was no way I could convince him that they were mere creatures of nature.

Since then I have spoken briefly on this subject, but only briefly. I am a pragmatic man, and I know only too well that God's children will never accept or understand the laws nature has designed to guide and help all gregarious mammals.

S INCE sheep have such limited talent to protect
  themselves from the adversities of life—predators, storms, etc.—nature has endowed them with other
means to continue in life; multiple births, and the ability to find and convert food.

   They are the most aggressive foragers of all farm
animals, and by far, the most reliant. If forced into the
pattern, they will nip grass to its roots, debark trees,
gnaw painted boards for their minerals, and breech most
any fence in their will to survive.

   On the other hand, sheep, if given the freedom they

desire and so rightly deserve, will treat the plants of the good earth with more respect than any other creature. It is not in their nature to be congested into herds of thousands. It is their nature to gently roam the hills in flocks of a couple hundred—to delicately choose small portions of every plant—to balance their own diet—to be free—to be left alone among their own kind—to disturb no other creature, and to give their life if it is necessary.

To call this pacific animal the "Cleft-footed Locust" is

Ewes and lambs
"nooned up."

to show lack of understanding of the gregarious nature of any mammal. One could say: it is to "understand" congested, urban man.

A Visit to Another Sheep Country

SEVERAL months ago I spent four weeks in the French Pyrenees with the Catalan peasants, working with them, observing them—most of the time, I have to admit, just sitting. I went to gather knowledge and only gathered sorrows. Not for them—their way of life was real and about as right as one could expect to find in this phony, cosmopolitan world. No, with sadness, I saw a preview of what is to come to our almost pure, uncongested American West.

I saw the "dudes" by the millions tramping over the peasant's ancient pastures, and many of the peasants welcoming and bargaining for the influx of new francs. And meter by meter, hectare by hectare—sure as the inherent greed of man—the land that once supported the Catalan's flocks and herds and an ancient, desirable way of life now supports only resorts, ski lifts, souvenir shops, and all the other clap-trap that goes with tourism.

There were flocks of sheep being guided past and around the asphalt routes that swarmed with the hither skitter of little cars. There were herds of Brown Swiss cattle in traffic jams with colonies of short-pantsed white-kneed kids. There were "dudes" buying gastronomic delights from a supermarket and, two doors away, watered milk from the peasant's stand. I saw huge pipes that carried the forces for hydroelectric power paralleling half-empty streams.

But above all, I saw human ignorance destroying and monopolizing the very soil that was the only vehicle for human sustenance that nature would ever supply. Soil to drive fast on...soil to play silly games on...soil to build chalets on...soil not to grow crops on.

Every evening all the animals would be driven down off the mountain and locked in the barn for the night.

A sheep dog turning the band.

101

Every morning they would be driven back up the mountain and herded all day with a vigilance that anticipated only the worst. Maybe this procedure was a habit of centuries. I don't know. Certainly, these peasants and the ancestors of these peasants had witnessed times I couldn't imagine. They no doubt had, in times past, fled with their flocks before marauding armies and stood in defense of their herds in times of occupation and famine as hungry urban hordes pressed them for portions of food.

The Catalan peasants never grazed the lambs with their mothers. As one peasant explained to me: when the lambs are shut up, the ewes would, even if they got separated from the band, return to the barn; also, the lambs fattened under this type of confinement were in great demand by the gourmet chefs.

Whatever the reasons, it is difficult for me to watch an animal void of freedom—any animal. It was doubly difficult for me to see little lambs confined to a barn for all their lives; to be born there, to grow to half their size there, to be slaughtered there. I would wander down about every other day to the barn where a peasant had his lambs shut up. I would peep through a crack in the ancient stucco and watch these poor little, manure-stained, exploited creatures trying to make the most of their "factory" environment. They had invented games, much like the ghetto kids in New York, that went up and down instead of length-wise. They would jump high in the air as one on a trampoline or a pogo stick; they would ride on each others backs like circus acrobats; they would play bunt-heads as best they could with only a two-foot run; but what was most pathetic was the sight of a small lamb trying to use his bigger cousin as a rock or bank to jump off of.

As I would walk back to the house, my mind could only think of the millions of caged chickens in America that had never scratched in a barnyard or chased a grasshopper; or the millions of pigs obliged to live their entire lives on concrete, pigs that had never wallowed in

A Catalan sheepherder.

a creek or rooted for angle worms on one of its banks. I could only curse at all the animal "factories" everywhere; not only at the ranchers and agri-businessmen who managed them, but especially at the effete urbans who demanded them.

Yes, cheap food is the panacea—conversion is the answer—roughage converted to protein—that the conversion is to involve life is of no importance. Yes, dear lovers of wildlife, protectors thereof, and all people with self-serving gaps in their ideals, the domestic animal was never wild and therefore deserves no freedom. God, how I would like to shove every urban head deep inside a slaughter house to hear the squeals, to see the fright, and to wade knee-deep in the blood pool.

Gastronomers, be damned!!

Epilogues and other Conclusions

AS I look around me at the old sheep sheds filling with cow manure, at old sheep fences being raised to constrain herds of Hereford and Angus steers, I can only kick at the dirt and curse at the changing times. There are many old sheepmen now adjusting their eye and corrals to the size of an old cow, stacking away the sheep panels, and above all, trying to think and act like cattlemen. This is not easy, since western sheepmen are of a different "breed."

At the turn of the century there were approximately 40 or 50 million breeding ewes in America. Today—less than 10 million, and the phase-out continues at an ever-increasing rate. in some western states, the sheep population dropped 10 to 20 percent this year alone. And there are no signals on the political and economic winds that presage any hope that the spiral might be arrested, and certainly none that it might be reversed.

There is no other alternative, in the face of the ever-increasing predator population—and consideration of another factor, the favorable cattle market—than to change a sheep ranching operation to one of cattle. In the last several years since the ban on the use of 1080, thousands of old-time sheep outfits who had stubbornly toughed it out for 50 years or longer, finally bent to that proverbial, back-breaking straw.

I personally have sold down to a small band that I can "hide" from time to time from the coyotes. But even these, I suppose—unless the present pattern is turned around—will go via the auction. At the present time, the closest neighbor with a band of sheep is 15 miles to the east, 20 miles to the north, 12 miles to the west, and 25 miles to the south. And, by conservative estimate, there are 200 coyotes in between. So it goes.

Last year, the yearly per capita consumption of lamb in America declined from 3.3. pounds to 2.7 pounds, and a large portion of that 2.7 pounds came from Australia and New Zealand. Within a few years (ranchers in Australia and New Zealand are also phasing out of the sheep business), lamb could become as rare as lobster and wool coats could replace mink coats as a status symbol. This is a slight exaggeration, but remember it was printed here first.

So, in this year of the crises, when the public is wishing they had voted for statesmen of contingency instead of "hacks" of the moment, the sheep industry is

occupied with its own little crisis. Of course, the politicians will conveniently remain unaware of this crisis, since with it goes only a few votes and a controversy that could cost them an election. But inter-related with this crisis is the impending food crisis due to hit America in the near future. And it will make the present energy crisis look like a Sunday outing in comparison.

I do not pose as an authority on this subject. No one is—the factors in the food equation are terribly complex and could involve another book. But from what I have experienced in my life in agriculture, I can only assume that American food production will, at best, remain constant. What will probably occur in the future is that the urban populations will be forced to adjust their eating habits to less meat and more "spuds." The majority of the spoiled, effete, city-oriented people of this world do not understand that a pound of meat-counter lamb (or beef) represents 40 pounds of hay and grass or 20 pounds of grain. It is a very expensive item to raise, and it is not just another plastic-wrapped bundle of bread or macaroni. It is a bundle of muscle that once contained life, but which is now camouflaged to hide all evidence of death.

I cannot feel sorry for most segments of urban America in any crisis, since they are responsible for constructing their own vulnerability. It was they who refused to pass laws—because of ignorance, greed, or complacency—that would have maintained millions of family farmers on the land. It was urban America that conveniently ignored the agricultural depression of the last 25 years; urban America that shut its eyes and hearts to the mass migration of millions of rural people from the country to city ghettos. It was the food-ignorant city dweller who, believing food and farmers went on forever, needlessly devoured millions and millions of acres of our best arable lands with urban expansion. It was the east-coast "dudes" who, 25 years ago, defeated

Secretary of Agriculture Brannan's plan to put American agriculture on an ecological, economic foundation that would have stabilized our food supplies for centuries to come.

As far as I am concerned, this segment of society, who treated food as a technological, capitalistic by-product and the people who produced it as expendable "hicks," deserve a few hunger pangs.

Eh bien!!

T HE winter is half gone and it had its own character: small portions of cold—the January thaw that entered early in the wake of violent Chinooks—and coyotes that came in packs, killing the older ewes one week and two-point buck deer the next.

I hope this doesn't herald dry weather and grasshoppers so long overdue.

A ewe dies, and the grass grows green and rank around her carcass. Years after her last fibers of wool have vanished into the earth, the other sheep will refrain from grazing there almost, it seems, in reverence to her death.

Epilogue

TEN years have passed since I wrote this book, and not much has changed.

The parity price for lambs and wool has dropped 6 or 7 percentage points...4 or 5 of my neighbors have sold their flocks...the coyotes are still out there, more numerous than ever...there are new anitbiotics and mutated bacteria to use on them...and the weather remains forever fickle.

...OH, WELL.